Science Says Yes

Also by Lynn McGee

Starting Over in Sunset Park (with José Pelauz)
Tracks
Sober Cooking
Heirloom Bulldog
Bonanza

SCIENCE SAYS YES

Poems by

Lynn McGee

Broadstone

Library of Congress Control Number 2024950614
ISBN 978-1-956782-90-5

Design by Ashley Johnson & Larry W. Moore

Cover artwork:
Amadeo de Souza-Carboso,
The Greyhounds (*Os Galgos*)

Broadstone Books
An Imprint of
Broadstone Media LLC
418 Ann Street
Frankfort, KY 40601-1929
BroadstoneBooks.com

Contents

Business & Technology

Happiness Is for Opportunists / 3
Betrayal Is Behind the Spread of Humans Around the World / 4
Lucy Fell: 12-Year-Old Hominin Lived 3.2 Million Years Ago and Is Known in Dinkinesh as, "You Are Marvelous." / 5
I Have a Past Life as an Early Human, and So Do You. / 6
We Know How to Reduce Earthquake Death. So Why Aren't We Doing It? / 7
Emotional AI Is no Substitute for Empathy / 9
Manage Your Energy, Not Your Time / 10
Who Is at Risk for Being Homeless? You are. / 11
Expect the Unexpected, Stay Vigilant and Ready to Respond / 12
What's Really Holding You Back? / 14
Longing Comes to Life: Mary Wollstonecraft Shelley Reflects on a Life Well Lived / 15
Differently Alert: A Rapport with Machines Gives Autistic Adults an Edge / 17
Tell Me One More Time, What to Do About Grief / 18
You're Never too Old to Have a Mentor / 19
The Pursuit of Happiness Could Be Making Us Miserable / 20
How to Fail Your Way to the Top / 21

Style

The Beauty of What Happens When Nothing Happens / 25
A Taste for Nostalgia: Why Our Food Memories Are So Powerful / 26
How to Recover from a Happy Childhood / 27
Tarantula in Black: Spider Named after Johnny Cash / 29
11,000 Americans Will Die Waiting for Organs This Year / 30
Some Early Childhood Experiences Shape Adult Life. But Which Ones? / 31
Bioluminescence Can Be Ours / 32
Bathing the Dog / 33
A Loneliness Epidemic Is Affecting a Staggering Number of American Adults / 34
Today's Witches Share the Powerful Link Between Makeup and Magic / 35

How Beauty Rituals Connect to Mental Health / 36
Small Acts of Kindness Are Frequent and Universal, Study Finds / 37
Can You Decorate and Clean Your Way to Happiness? Science Says Yes / 38

Climate & Environment

Lethal Weapons May Have Given Early Humans Edge Over Neanderthals / 41
Lake Mead: See What Extreme Drought Has Exposed / 42
Rampant Wildfires Once Led to Global Mass Extinctions, Scientists Say. Could it Happen Again? / 43
Six Signs Your Spirit Guide Is Here / 44
How to Rewire Your Traumatized Brain / 45
Biking It Off / 47
Global Warming Is Disrupting the Birds and Bees / 48
Animals Will Take Over the Earth After We Eradicate Ourselves / 49
Astronauts Face Extended Time on Space Station, NASA Says / 50
Space Junk Pollutes the Stratosphere as we Befoul the Last Frontier / 52
Why the Modern World Is Bad for Your Brain / 54
Your Crushing Anxiety About the Climate Crisis Is Normal / 55
Why Women Are Key to Solving the Climate Crisis / 56

Opinion

Welcome to the Age of Anger / 59
What Animals Can Teach Us About Being Human / 60
Scientists Have Finally Found Out Why People Love Each Other / 61
Sweet Concrete Dream: Skate Culture Transcends Sellout Culture / 62
The Meat Paradox: Why People Can Love Animals—and Eat Them / 64
Everything I Learned About Forgiveness, I Learned From my Dog / 65
You Are Made of Stardust / 66
Why Starting Over Can Be the Best Thing for You / 67
Everything Looks Better in the Fleeting Beauty of the Golden Hour / 68

Acknowledgments / 70

Business & Technology

Happiness Is for Opportunists

I pass my second decapitated bird of the day,
gray dove with a ragged red throat.

Maybe she was sipping water trapped between
paving squares on the sidewalk, a cat saw
his opportunity and pounced.

Opportunists live longer, by their own design.
When wolf populations are low,
they mate with coyotes.

When wolf populations are high,
they kill coyotes.

Betrayal Is Behind the Spread of Humans Around the World

A moving van backed up beeping to the curb.
The corrugated door rolled out of sight.

Gorillas raised their heads from hammocks
that swung from the ribbed ceiling.

They blinked at the light.

One silverback shuffled to the edge of the open
hold and dropped his elegant, leathery hand
to the sidewalk.

He hopped to the pavement with easy grace,
and gamboled down the block.

The truck driver scrambled after him and stood
shoulders relaxed, head down, stroking
the gorilla's shaggy arm.

I was in a crowd watching, and felt a light tap —
the person next to me held out his hand.

Someone else softly stroked my back, and we
followed the driver's lead, touched each other
calmly, breathing slowly.

We enacted harmony, simulated love.
We created a tableau meant to be read as
Trust us, when we should have
yelled *Run*.

Lucy Fell:
12-Year-Old Hominin Lived 3.2 Million Years Ago and Is Known in Dinkinesh as, "You Are Marvelous."

Imagine the only safe place to sleep is up. Below is the surging
world of fangs and rot. Weapons haven't happened yet,
and tools are valued less than the nimble strength
it takes to scale a trunk, quickly.

Lucy fell. She was sleeping in a nest that crumbled beneath her.
She was startled and lost her grip, when an eagle wheeled
close. She was inching down one branch, standing and holding
another overhead when she slipped, kicking
like a hanged man, and dropped.

She was arboreal. She was terrestrial. She had long arms
and the curved hands of a climber, but the big toe of a walker,
a paddle for balance, and what she wasn't, was avian —

no webs of hollow bones flared from her shoulders
like a pair of fans that could have snapped open and saved
her — and she landed feet first, shoulder blade snapping
and the severed bone biting down, organs bursting
like eggs dropped from a roof.

She bled out quickly, saturating the ground.
She lay undisturbed as the earth's skull split apart
and shifted, its surface crowded by her descendants
and a team of grad students in jeans and T-shirts
who whisk through sand

to find her. Who assemble with great care, the crumbling
segments of bone. Who scour with lasers, where marrow
had lived. Who drop to their knees when minerals
born in stars flicker marvelous in the light.

I Have a Past Life as an Early Human, and So Do You.

Splash your face with cold water and wake the early
human brain curled at the base of your modern brain,

the limbic cortex coddled in furrows and sloshing in brine,
a nugget of neurons once allotted a lot of fuel just to flip

the switch to fight or take flight and save us from a bear
that sauntered solid as a truck, a lion whose jaw could

crack your skull in one bite. The brain's ancient root
is a fist that fuels the nerves and muscle needed to leap

aside, under, down or through, when a bully blocks
your path in a city park or leers down at your metal desk

in a cubicle pinned with your children's photos.
The ancient brain gives you strength to hurl rocks

if a raptor sweeps into your cave, clutches a shrieking
infant in its talons and labors across the sky

We Know How to Reduce Earthquake Deaths. So Why Aren't We Doing It?

My first earthquake rippled the plush aisle
of a movie theater in Hollywood.

I froze and took a wide stance, arms out,
as if surfing to the end of days.

We laughed about it on the drive home, unaware
that the I-10 crosses the San Andreas fault
a dozen times.

I moved to New York and forgot about that night
till workers dug for pipes and steel cable,
and a neighbor's lawn collapsed.

A man tumbled into the jaws of darkness.

Someone threw him a harness and he swung
suspended from a pole that spanned
the gaping hole.

News vans lined the street. It wasn't
an earthquake, it was a warning.

The earth's tectonic plates grind up against each
other like drunks passing in a narrow hallway.

Eventually, they fight.

A seismic shift gears up and crystals gnash,
embedded below ground.

They release sparks that shoot up through the surface
and scatter across the sky.

Sheet lightning, streamers, blue light join the surge
of souls released from the rubble of buildings in Haiti,
Turkey, Indonesia, Morocco, the Philippines,
India, China, Iran and San Francisco,
the San Fernando Valley.

Barges carry wreckage down rivers clotted with debris.
Bulldozers shove bent steel and carnage into mounds.

Even as the surface of the earth is pushed back
into place, laborers pressure-blast sand
to widen crevices beneath a pasture
in Oklahoma, a field in Pennsylvania.

This gouging and forcing open eases the flow
of fossil fuel to a wellbore sunk through bedrock
hot enough to cook a roast.

An oil drill squats on the choppy waters
of the Gulf of Mexico.

Its elbows and wheels complicate the horizon.
Some would call it beautiful,
against the red sky.

Emotional AI Is No Substitute for Empathy

Jesus knew it wouldn't be viruses that would
wipe us out, wildfires or nuclear war.

He knew it would be a lack of empathy,
and tried to guide us in the other direction:
Do unto others, as you would have them
do unto you.

Now, AI has been made in our image,
and it lacks what we lack.

Scientists say, *Give it sensors placed*
in the environment, vulnerable
to forces it can't control.

Teach it suffering is unacceptable,
in any solution set.

AI thrives despite its flaws.

It carries on — like any monarch, any god
dogged by unregulated lust, hubris,
greed.

And then there are the humans,
eaten by their children.

Manage Your Energy, Not Your Time

Dystopic movies normalize dystopia. Fast food
normalizes fast lunches. High heels normalize
compliance, and the crowded subway
normalizes subjugation.

You commute home, eroded by the day's
negotiations.

Your living room darkens and the yellow sky
goes indigo.

Silence surges over you, interrupted now and then
by the whoosh and clack of elevator doors
sliding open, closed.

Your neighbors' footsteps rise and fade
in a doppler pattern down the hallway.

Cells begin to recognize each other, in your
re-integrating self.

When enough time has passed, you turn on
the light.

Who Is at Risk for Being Homeless? You Are.

At the stop light, a young man in jeans, a tight
white t-shirt, shaved head and muscled arms rolls
his wheelchair alongside my car and rattles
a red-and-white bucket from KFC.

He pounds the driver's-side window with his fist.
I stare at the hatchback of the car in front of me.

Walking to the restaurant, I see him again.

Disgust crumples his face and he turns his head
away, spins his wheelchair and speeds off.

A waiter hands me a menu heavy with laminated pages —
À la Carte, World's Best Bloody Mary, Apple Baked
Muffins, plates pillowed with omelets, opulent
pancakes dribbled with syrup and dollar amounts
tucked here and there, in bold.

Expect the Unexpected, Stay Vigilant and Ready to Respond

A piano crescendo blasts from the cell phone of a man
striding toward me with his well-oiled musculature,
neon-green tank top and shorts —

No, I'm wrong. It's a recital in full swing
at the private school down the block.

A white tent has been erected in its field. My dog's head
pans back and forth, tracking a kid on a banana bike
in its parking lot.

We shift our focus when a jeep sputters up the road —
not a yellow Wrangler with flames painted down
its sides, not a purple Cherokee with yellow trim —

but a vintage Army jeep, bulldog-wide and mud-caked,
side panels a dark green that's almost black,
antlers mounted on its hood.

It slams to a stop and the passenger hops out to aim
his phone while the driver guns it up the steep
slope along the shoulder.

He hits the brakes at maximum tilt and waves
his beer can out the window, grinning
for the shot.

My dog's gaze is locked. She's not from around here,
and the spectacle, I'm guessing, doesn't quite match
what she knows — Big-wheel truck. Flat-bed
trailer. Dirt bikes. ATVs.

I'm not from here, either, and peer down the street
for anything else unexpected, my switch to high alert
so casual, I almost don't notice.

What's Really Holding You Back?

A circus elephant is cinched
into a howdah.
The sequined saddle lurches
and jangles with each
leaden step.
Her eyes are hooded,
lashes white, and the spotlight
makes them pink.
A terrier leaps to her trunk —
she lifts him to her back.
A beach ball rolls on stage —
she sways, and swats it back.
She misses the kind touch
of another elephant's trunk.
She misses walking in a space
that is not a circle.
She hurls herself into
the bleachers,
smears the front row
in a mash of organs, bones
and blood. *It's happening,*
I tell someone standing
beside me. *How long*
could she pretend to be
something she's not?

Longing Comes to Life: Mary Wollstonecraft Shelley Reflects on a Life Well Lived

Cook let me put my arm into the cavity of a goose. I felt
the suck of death and slickness of life, two sides of the same

coin. It can happen fast — I made a corpse of my mother,
when I slid from her body, and father banned me

from his library. I taught myself to read, studied the city
around me, watched it nurse its theaters like a sow

with a new brood. On some stages, men died clattering
to the floor and velvet curtains swung shut. On some stages,

men lay sprawled on the draining table, torsos split like barrels
dropped to the dock. I am not among the audience of scholars

on tiered seats rising in a circle, but I know of the ambition
at its center, blood siphoned from a sheep to a boy,

from one great, panting mastiff to another. Women fare
no better — a hook dismantles the infant wedged

in its mother's red canal. My three babies were born whole.
They had cashmere scalps, and cooled in my arms. I had

no one but myself to blame. No one made me follow
the first man who saw me clearly, who prized the forest

teeming inside me. I lavished my story upon him. It started
with a ship's mast and ropes glazed in ice: That which freezes,

might shatter. That which is electrified back to life, glides
across a glacier and stands towering on a sled, whipping

his dogs. I passed down to my creature the curse of longing
for what is withheld by others. I carry my lover's heart

in a pouch. It rattles hard as a peach pit next to my heart,
which ripens on its branch.

Differently Alert: A Rapport With Machines Gives Autistic Adults an Edge

He doesn't make eye contact, the nurse reports
of my nephew who is limp with sedation, lips slack,
ventilator wheezing on his behalf, inflating his lungs
in a rhythm both amiable and stern. *He looks right*
past me, she says gently. *He's probably unaware*
of his surroundings. We thank her, too polite
to point out the monitor's appeal, just behind her,
neon green zig-zagging across its screen. We don't
bring to her attention, the splendor of syringe pumps
stacked in a tower, the elegant tangle of cables,
polished elbows of pipe. My nephew, who took
the door off the stove before he could walk,
who faked seizures to score an ambulance ride
and be rolled into that luminous cavern of tools,
stares past the nurse at an alluring silver dial,
a corrugated blue tube, and is unbothered at being
part machine now himself, almost fitting in.

Tell Me, One More Time, What to Do About Grief

When the familiar feels barbed, when it scalds,
let the unfamiliar be your solace,

as chunky paperbacks were for me, blood-soaked
covers fanning across the sale bin
at an all-night Walmart,

as was country music — not crossover hits
from the Dixie Chicks or Rosanne Cash, but songs
that twanged and squalled at the bottom

of the chart, salty with static from a radio
kept low, songs that made a circle of low flame
around me.

You're Never Too Old to Have a Mentor

Lou Reed was in high school, once,
and he wanted to play for the coach,
the straightest dude he knew,
standing right for him,
all the time. Rest in peace,
our fallen coaches. Give us strength
to walk in the forest without intention,
to honor the engines of our bodies
and shake loose any stray, combustive
materials. To adjust our coolant levels,
rest quietly and start up easily,
as our coaches taught us.
To up our game, as the trail rises
and dips. To *send this one out,*
when you're all alone and lonely.
Winter is for storage. Spring is when
the earth restarts. Clusters of light
scab the low hills.

The Pursuit of Happiness Could Be Making Us Miserable

I engage in the pursuit of happiness like a bicycle
crashing into a barn — and with accidental success.

I enter a state of happiness when I'm just back
from the dog run, rinsing mud from tennis balls
under the spigot's hot spray till each
yellow orb is pure again.

I smoke some stale weed from last winter,
and pockets of emotion thaw in my sternum.

I begin to lighten. My footsteps evaporate.
I create a place for happiness to land —
I'm a landing strip.

I fill the void space in every garden
put before me.

Happiness leans against the wall, amused
at my efforts, waiting to be noticed.

How to Fail Your Way to the Top

In sixth grade they taught us the dangers of smoking,
and our class had a poster contest.

We sat quietly grunting at our desks, crayons
indenting white paper.

I drew a man sitting up in bed, "X"s for eyes,
the headboard a tombstone blaring *RIP*,
and a caption warning *Smoke in Bed,*
Wake up Dead.

I understood the illogic of waking up dead,
but no other phrase gave the same punch.

I was in love with the stylish impossible,
a love that still inspires me to choose right,
choose wrong.

I marvel at the earth's frothy curve,
every time I fall.

Style

The Beauty of What Happens When Nothing Happens

I will never tire of seedless grapes, or news
of aliens, the discovery of a splinter of bone
from the femur of an early human.

I will never love, yet never hate refilling
the humidifier, lugging the jug of water back
to its base near my bed,

and I will always have an effortless tolerance
for speed bumps that rise on my street
like new graves.

What solace — the ordinary, the beautiful
unremarkable.

What great fortune, to glide through our days,
buffered by its presence.

A Taste for Nostalgia: Why Food Memories Are So Powerful

Lightning ignited a band of woolly oxen huddled
beneath a tree and charred meat hit the menu,
sending more fuel to human brains and less
to their slippery, churning gut.

Fast-forward a few millennia and a child holds up
a white plate, tilts it at her mouth to drink the blood
from a steak, while forty million cattle swing
by their hind legs, entrails squeegeed
into a trough, and nine billion chickens flap
in water laced with lightning —

bringing this story full circle, back to the spark,
the smoking flesh.

Crickets crave grease, and so do we, gastric acid
activated by a street vendor's skewered chicken
on an open flame, the Halal truck at lunch hour,
charred hunk of lamb sizzling on a spit —

and I would give anything to see my father at the grill,
basting rib-eyes, wielding the stainless-steel tongs
in one hand, frosty can of beer in the other.

How to Recover from a Happy Childhood

Childhood was flip-flops sticking to hot tar
and smacking back down.

It was the wrath of mothers, tracks of purple
half-moons dug by fingernails,
up a child's arm.

It was the Formica table wiped down after dinner,
a sleepy teenager wringing out her sponge,
standing at the sink and singing quietly
out the window to an empty backyard.

The curious drama of childhood coursed around
a first grader with a dead squirrel in his lunchbox,
and the dying 13-year-old down the block,
her bruised, slender hand waving slowly
behind a screen door.

It was someone's dad perp-walked in handcuffs
down the sidewalk lined with tulips to the cop car
at the curb, and the stage whispers of grownups:
White collar crime, the highest form of vice.

It was the half-built house we snuck out to,
sweet scent of sawdust and a mattress
on the plywood floor, an 11-year-old's
cigarette breath and fruity scent
of a strange boy's hair.

It was bawdy jokes about the FBI, *Female Body
Inspector,* and girls with hard knots of breasts,
tugging at their first *Over-the-Shoulder-
Boulder-Holder*.

The past is a wrecked ship on the floor of the ocean
and we glide above it, raking the depths to find
the moments that made us.

What a spectacle, that sunken vessel,
even as it dissolves.

Tarantula in Black: Spider Named After Johnny Cash

Johnny Cash sang from the blond hi-fi in our house,
and he wore black *for the poor and beaten-down*
on the hungry side of town. He was the same age
as my father, who was coltish and tall, and cast
his fishing rod with a quick, casual whip.

Someone who has the power to do so, name a just-found
streak of rock, a block of onyx pulling darkness,
then releasing it as light — name that rock
after my father, with his quiet flair.

Name a new species of migrating tern — forked tail
splitting with never-before-seen snap and fan —
name that species for my nephew, with his unruly
genes, his differently split ways.

Let some newly discovered, indissoluble speck —
neither somber neutrino nor high-spirited electron —
let that particle be named after his mother,
my sister, her flash intact.

11,000 Americans Will Die Waiting for Organs This Year

Doctors in a hospital in South China crowd the hallway
in their green scrubs and masks, surrounding a boy
on a gurney, tucked under a sheet, his brain
a city with a darkened grid.

The doctors bow low, three times — to heaven,
to earth, and to all living things, including the boy;
his bone marrow, kidneys, heart and lungs
about to relearn their purpose, waking
in the bodies of strangers.

Don't judge too harshly, those of us who have ripped down
the flyer taped to the door of a loved one's room
in ICU: *Donate an Organ, Save a Life.*

Forgive us, those who kept the body alive too long
to make its parts of any use, for being slow
to learn when to stand guard,
and when to bow.

Some Early Childhood Experiences Shape Adult Life. But Which Ones?

I was raised by Texans, learned to water ski
when I was seven that summer we stayed in tents
around a lake, smell of bacon and cigarettes
in the morning, my aunt at the campfire
stirring eggs in an iron skillet.

I loved my ukulele shaped like an electric guitar,
stretch pants red with foot straps, horse figurines
herded on my dresser. I loved to memorize —
the Gettysburg Address, Crest Pledge, Shakespeare:
Then be some other name! and I loved
Greek mythology, the lurid pettiness of gods —
Kronos, gobbling his own infants; Hera, infested
with jealousy and Dionysus, whose hedonism thrilled
a child discouraged from excess —

but *The Wizard of Oz*, I loved most of all.
Auntie Em twisted her apron, plump
like my grandmother twisting tomatoes
off the vine, watching the sky.

Waves of homesickness hit me, lying
on my stomach in front of the TV console
with its black knobs and green glass.
Those waves, I feel them still.

Bioluminescence Can Be Ours

When the shark looks up, he sees stars. Taurus gores
the night sky. Ursus ambles toward morning. A squid glides
past, legs trailing in the cold sea, underside lit with radiant
bacteria the predators below confuse for constellations
rippling across the sky. Humans know better. We scrape
microbes from the luminous bellies of cephalopods,
harvest a gel that lights a street. We fill a syringe, inject
leaves with the sparkling genetic dust of eels,
and birds veer from a park's fabricated glow. We clap
on fireflies and trap them flaming in jars, and sometimes,
in our haste, snuff out the life, but not the light
of insects whose green neon smears up to our elbows.
Even as children, we seize what shines.

Bathing the Dog

My father is bathing his old bird dog
in the backyard.
She is either very wise
or very dim, stiff as a guard,
one brittle leg deep in a bucket,
his big hand gingerly closing the hinge
that allows it to bend, rise
and settle cracked leather pads on concrete
warmed by sun.
She rattles her collar,
water snapping in sheets,
long ears slapping,
and he towels her off brusquely
as he did, long ago, for me, and for you,
who was pale and quick,
who shared his happy regard
for logic, who had his narrow face
and sharp chin, eyes gray
as overcast sky, wild hair tied back
without ceremony or care,
your ashtray gleaming, now,
on a patio bench, crystal
licked by sun and sputtering
light, powerful in its uselessness,
his good dog rubbed down
and released.

A Loneliness 'Epidemic' Is Affecting a Staggering Number of American Adults

They pass me and my dog; two boys, maybe twelve
and ten. The taller one holds a football with one hand
and smacks it with the other, feigning
the wind-up to a pass.

They both wear yarmulkes embroidered with flourishes
of gold and scarlet thread.

Their glossy dark hair is sheered close on the sides,
foreheads swept with long bangs that the younger one
tosses out of his eyes like a jaded, stylish woman.

The boys turn down a side street and a startled pigeon
flaps out of their way. My dog stops to stare after
them, sniffing the air.

When I was their age, we debated the merits
of superpowers. I wanted invisibility, to see
without being seen, to go where I was
not allowed — not the gift of flight.

It's our last walk of the night. It's Christmas eve,
it's my birthday, it's Valentine's Day,
it's the fourth of July.

The sun is low and my long shadow merges
with my dog's spidery cut-out. Our two-headed
likeness dances down the sidewalk.

Today's Witches Share the Powerful Link Between Makeup and Magic

Behind the beaten metal door and wavy mirror,

on the narrow rusting shelves I find invisible

protection, a substance that rebuilds, restores

and refreshes my life. I find an invitation to take

what I need and apply it daily, liberally.

There are gentle reminders to wear a long-

sleeved shirt, hat and sunglasses, to check

the quality seal and avoid inhalation.

I avail myself of a proven strength system,

an Alpine breeze, instant sleek.

I seize an infallible foundation.

How Beauty Rituals Connect to Mental Health

The art and science of beautifying hair, skin and nails
attracts persuasive problem solvers,
the quick thinkers among us,

chemists who snap the light sensors in their retinas,
read the color bouncing off a surface and craft
a strategy around it.

In high school there were kids who took college prep,
boys with combed-back hair in automotive,
and girls in cosmetology.

Their beehive hairdos bobbed like planets
above the lunchroom crowd.

They wore nylons under their gym shorts while
other girls pulled up knee socks on the gymnasium's
glossy court.

We stayed out of each other's way — the pot heads,
the popular girls, the girls with teased hair,
the cheerleaders, the ones who would never
leave their hometown, the ones
who would never return.

We passed in the crowded hallway polite as birds
who sense their flock in a fog, whose wings
never touch.

I didn't know then, that cosmetology employs
the laying on of hands.

A person feels heard, when someone palpates
their scalp.

Small Acts Of Kindness Are Frequent And Universal, Study Finds

They pulled over to the shoulder — a green John Deere
tractor with giant back tires, a dozen sedans and pickups,
a patrol car with black doors and white hood,
its roof lights blinking, silent.

They glided off-road to the grassy shoulder of an East Texas
highway flanked with barbed wire and rusty acres
of wheat —

all to let our limo pass and make way for cars that followed
us to the cemetery with its crunchy brown grass
and colossal live oak dominating the horizon,
holding our family in its shadow.

Can You Decorate and Clean Your Way to Happiness? Science Says Yes.

It's comforting to pivot in the galley kitchen,
slide the skillet into its slot, toss the spoons

in one rectangle and forks in the other.
The utensils' collective weight flies

from my hand and I am deft, ergonomically sound,
enacting a choreography as old as racing

through rain, a pack of us, feral with youth,
barefoot, t-shirts sopping wet,

leaping porch to porch in the warm,
lascivious rain.

Climate & Environment

Lethal Weapons May Have Given Early Humans Edge over Neanderthals

I admit they have appeal, the accoutrements of hunting —

the fur pouch, leather ties, kidney-shaped straw basket

for fish. The bushcraft gear. The orange vest

and windproof gloves with a slot for your trigger finger.

The high-carbon, stainless steel knife — objects worthy

of the drive to overcome, to outsmart, to never go hungry

or turn away from danger, to call the shots, to win.

Lake Mead: See What Extreme Drought Has Exposed

I yearn to float on my back, open my arms and trail them
back and forth through the tepid currents of a lake.

I yearn for a lake to slow me down, not as opposition —
like the crowded subway, or heavy traffic — but as
the short-bristled brush slowed down my dog,
that first time I dragged it the length of her spine
and she stood in place, putting all her energy
into processing pleasure.

That's the kind of slow we need, the kind that puts
the brakes on pesticides surging into waterways.

Here's what we have in its absence — Lake Mead
a jagged vein across the orange landscape.

Bodies and cars surface, as the water shrinks.

The critical mass it would take to turn this drought
around, won't happen, and the lake gives more
than it gets.

We shave paths across the earth. I catch myself
accelerating, alongside everyone else.

Rampant Wildfires Once Led To Global Mass Extinction, Scientists Say. Could It Happen Again?

If you drop water from the sky, it evaporates
before it hits the flames. Silica in soil turns to glass.
Zombie fires — the undead of fires — bide their time
and erupt from underground like a rage-addled
Persephone, clawing every tree with flame.

If you miss your father, it's because he's not here
to tell you the fires won't take us down.

The first time I escaped death, I was seven,
floating in a crouch, water skis pointed forward,
both hands on the plastic handle, waiting to rise
and cut my wake into a bass lake in Arkansas.

The boat's motor revved. Rainbows of gasoline
shuddered on the surface of the water.

The orange tow rope made a wide loop that snapped
around my waist and I was yanked deep beneath
the water's glittering surface.

The last thing I saw was my father's face
at the stern, his puzzled look.

If you miss your father, it's because every buffer
between you and danger is wearing thin.

Fire follows the earth's curve. Firefighters load into
helicopters and work 20-hour shifts. A smoke jumper
parachutes to the jaws of hell. Pine needles hiss
as they edge toward ignition.

Six Signs Your Spirit Guide Is Here

It buoyed me, that dream of my childhood home
with its deep-breathing lawn and white gardenia
in a snifter, infusing the air with hope.

All my lost people drifted through its hallways
with their easy, familiar postures; their easy,
familiar laughs.

A breeze passed through them and passed through
me. Our bones whistled. Ribbons of long hair lifted,
as if sniffing the air.

The landscape mirrored a painting I grew up with,
white barns on rounded green hills like a woman
lying on her side, asleep.

The painting made no sense — *Barns should be red,*
I thought as a child. But now I like them white.

How to Rewire Your Traumatized Brain

I woke one morning last winter and asked Siri
what the temperature was: *82 degrees.*

The world had gone from freezing to balmy,
overnight.

Full of groggy joy, I opened a window,
and cold rolled over me as if I were standing
at the open door of a walk-in freezer.

I felt pranked by AI, as I went about my day.

My dog and I headed out, and delicate sprays
of hail cooled the back of my neck,
made her fur glisten.

We arrived at the pond and sunlight pierced
the clouds, ignited its surface.

A pair of mallards floated touching each other,
wings tucked tight, shellacked by sun —

one with a green, iridescent throat, the other
the color of dried grass.

They glided on the water's surface, hinged
to their own image.

My dog and I stood silent at the pond's
muddy bank.

There are days we make false starts,
wish for foolish things —

and then there are the ducks,
the beautiful ducks.

Biking It Off

Claritin, caffeine, cannabis — I'm self-medicating
through a breakup, inhaling late-summer musk that rises
from a mud path packed flat in a forest drunk

with the deep-summer saturation of glucose and green,
muffled pop of a tennis ball counter-balanced
by the whack of a cricket bat. I'm wearing

a helmet and my skull heats up, my heart fills, all four
chambers pulling tight as a rowing crew leaving
its long V down a river. I'm coasting

on the inertia of my own mass. I'm a dog with its
head out the car window, heading home, where
a breeze laps my balcony and I stretch out

on a yoga mat, looking up at the racing sky. Low sun
ignites the distant ridge of trees. Air cools fast
but surfaces are still warm, the food chain

in full swing. Birds dive with expert haste. Insects
breed as fast as they can line up sperm packets
and ducts, sometimes midair.

Global Warming Is Disrupting the Birds and Bees

A sea turtle digs with her back legs, digits fused
into a paddle.

Sand sprays in an arc behind her.

Her cloaca opens like a flower and the slick,
tear-shaped eggs slide down and drop.

She scoops sand over the clutch, drags a jumble
of seaweed to mask her nest and trundles
back into the surf.

Fist-sized fetuses take shape in the trapped heat
of their shells.

Males are baked too long and morph into females
whose yellow eyes will scan the cloudy currents,
one day, for mates they outnumber
a hundred to one.

When two sea turtles lock together, the male
holds on with elegant, elongated claws.

Other males nip his tail, his stubby back legs.
Ribbons of blood waft up around him,
but he keeps tight, his grip that took millions
of years to perfect.

Animals Will Take Over the Earth, After We Eradicate Ourselves

A wasp goes limber in the sauna
of a kitchen window,
is coaxed ambling onto the corner
of an index card, carried sailing
to that place where the universe opens
and with magnificent greed,
closes on its bumbling descent,
snow melting on impact,
hardening like teeth on six legs
swimming, then curling
as it sinks into white,
sun exploding in the distance,
churning paper nest
attached like an organ
to great ribs of the attic.

Astronauts Face Extended Time on Space Station, NASA Says

Thrusters malfunctioned. That's the hold up. If all else
fails, we can catch a ride home on a SpaceX capsule
scheduled to pass by next year.

Meanwhile, my sleeping closet is a perfect fit,
and I don't mind the flashes of light when I close
my eyes, cosmic rays surging through my retinas.

The coffee's not bad, either; squeezed from
a plastic bag, sucked through a straw.
Meals are ready to go or just add water,
humidity harvested from our showers,
breath and urine.

We've got hot sauce, we've got condiments.
Yes, I saw *Alien*, and No, we don't have weapons,
though Russian cosmonauts stow a gun on board,
in case they crash-land in Siberia and hungry
bears shoulder through snow drifts,
to find them. Cosmonauts smoke
cigarettes in space, too,

but not us, not the Americans, though we have
other comforts; Oreos, M&Ms and Jello cups.
I have my Swiss Army knife, Girl Scout cookies,
books on tape and a digital piano.

Dozens of engineers and scientists track us
from the ground, and watch us through cameras
if we give Houston *permission to come aboard.*

We're in charge of our days and it's safety first,
all the way. The Israelis have lost one astronaut
in space; Soviets four, Americans thirteen.

We had the Challengers, the Columbia disasters,
but no one yet — forget what Hollywood dreams up —
has snapped their tether as they floated,

gingerly feeling their way around the outer wall
of a space station, wielding a pistol-grip
hand drill, making a repair.

The body cut loose in space would petrify
in a snap, its inner oceans boiling.

It would drift into a gravity field and ignite,
reborn as a star locked in an infinite,
elliptical course.

It's worth it to see Earth the first time, from space.

My dream is that the wealthiest of the wealthy
in their flip flops and straw hats will travel
to space for kicks and see the Earth
as I have,

that their love for the unanchored Earth
will surge as they watch it float soundlessly
with its tender, blue, gauzy wrap,
and they will redirect their funds,
to save it.

Space Junk Pollutes the Stratosphere as We Befoul the Last Frontier

You're standing at the kitchen counter snipping tags
off a pile of placemats and running shorts
the FedEx driver dropped at your doorstep —

all of which will be cast out with crumbled
Styrofoam, egg cartons and jars, your neighbors'
broken vacuum and computer monitor —

discards drifting to a landfill teeming with gulls,
to a barge stacked with bales of trash,
to a mile-wide island of garbage
bobbing on the open sea.

The more we have, the more we cast aside.
Space junk — discarded rocket boosters,
satellites used as target practice — circle the earth
like shooting stars.

The orange sky ripples with chemicals.
Particulates ferry viruses to nest in the lungs
of the infirm, the underweight —

like a boy in laceless Adidas. Like his brother
in a UCLA sweatshirt, cut sleeveless. They wrestle
over a bent spoon scavenged from a mountain
of slush bulldozed outside Delhi.

Trash coagulates in a river lined with tin roofs
in Cambodia. A monsoon soaks the landfill
near Manila, and an avalanche of trash crushes
the shantytown below.

A trash truck idles on a cobblestoned street
in New York City.

I shift into park and a sanitation worker in orange gloves
gives me a quick wave. I give him a thumbs-up
and he rolls a dumpster to a giant, hydraulic fork
that heaves it up and empties it into the hopper,
where a compactor does its staggering work.

Why the Modern World Is Bad for Your Brain

Stop trying to sell me running shoes, dog beds
and diet plans.

Stop riding the air current to my face,
stop infecting my lungs.

I'm talking to you — consumer trackers, airborne
virus.

Stop making my teeth ache. Stop throwing
off my car's alignment. Stop chewing the wires
to my engine block and stabbing
my lower back —

be gone, cold front, pot hole, hungry rat
and herniated disc.

Stop corroding my resolve, Anxiety.
Stop waking me at 3 a.m., Insomnia.

I've had it, I'm not having it, I've had
enough, I'm done.

I rise up with my reasonable request.

Your Crushing Anxiety About the Climate Crisis Is Normal

Just as cells live inside our bodies,
unable to fathom scale,

the universe is a cell that lives
in the body of something larger —

and it thrives when we thrive,
feels the earth falter, when we fail.

Our planet's surface isn't a self-healing mat,
criss-crossed lines made by Exacto knives,
filled in by morning.

Give our planet time to knit back together,
I say, hoping to convince my gods.

Give us time to pull this off.

Why Women Are Key to Solving the Climate Crisis

I want a raven to land on the railing

of my balcony while I'm stretched out

on the chaise lounge drinking a pale ale.

I want the raven to move its gaze up

and down my body, and when it determines

I am neither food nor foe, I want the raven

to push off and unfurl its opulent black wings,

and instantly forget me.

Opinion

Welcome to the Age of Anger

A woman I knew went to a recycling center
where they let her smash glass with a mallet,
goggles slippery with sweat.

The weight of a baseball bat would do it for me.
The heft of the lid on the back of the toilet
would fuel a good swing — but what

would be the target? What object of impact
would explode with enough force to suck
the darkness right out of me?

The trick is letting the darkness stay.
Give the darkness your key. Stir charcoal
and animal fat together and dab a tribute
to darkness, on the wall of your cave.

Pick a spot where the sun hits each day.
Watch it laser through the dark.
Watch the dark change cell by cell.
Feel it settle inside you.

What Animals Can Teach Us About Being Human

If I had what animals have, I would rise on my hind legs,
skate on the water's surface like a basilisk, send an arc
of spray as if angling my skis around a lake like my mother,
who never got her hair wet, who let go of the orange handle
and glided with quiet dignity into the shallow beach.

If I had what animals have, my retina would bloom
with more cones than the human eye is meant to hold,
and I would see not just the hues my species relies on —
wine-red berries, yellow pears, blue plums —
but colors shimmering at a frequency
having only to do with pleasure.

I would know when to fight, when to activate flight.
I would regenerate lost limbs, reallocate my energy
in a more strategic way, sleep one radiant hemisphere
of my brain at a time.

If I had what animals have, my bones would hollow out.
I would fly and when I'd had enough, I would curl
into myself like a jellyfish bobbing on death's
maternal wave. I would retract my tentacles
and revert to some long-past, natal state,
sink to the ocean floor where I began.

I would wait there and savor the soft dark.
I would give thanks to those who made me —
the lizard clawing out a trench and squeezing eggs
from her cloaca, the starfish shooting a cloud
of cells into the water, the mother who infused me
in her womb — I would thank them all,
and then restart my life.

Scientists Have Finally Found Out Why People Love Each Other

Seventeenth-century Saxon miners called it
Wolfram, the mountain's streak of ore that flashed

fangs and set off slagging, devoured cliffs,
they wrote, *like a wolf devours sheep*. It still snakes

the Alps, and it takes heat rivaling the sun's
blazing surface, to make it boil. Stir in carbon

and it percolates, writhes in ovens and spins
like sugar into strands that lace an electric grid,

that light up a skyline sharp as spikes on a lizard's
spine, my apartment embedded in clouds

and holding me deep in a gold leather chair,
my lover kneeling elegant as a priest, a woman

who wields her height like a boat wields its sail,
a woman in wolf's clothing — *Wolfram,*

my Valentine holding out a small red box,
a tungsten ring inlayed with blue carbon fiber,

lighting my hand with its teeth.

Sweet Concrete Dream: Skate Culture Transcends Sellout Culture

On weekends, we took her kid to skateboard lessons
in a warehouse resplendent with half-pipes —
plywood ramps curling up to heaven.

Corrugated doors that had once rattled open
for semi-trailers were airbrushed
in flaming hearts,

three generations of teeming, dockside labor
extinguished in one good long recession
and turned Tweener Heaven,

some kid sliding down a ramp on his belly,
his instructor in long braids flipping a water bottle
with delicate finesse as he demo's,
again and again,

how to pivot, whip the nose of the board
and point it toward home.

First, tie your shoes, how many times I gotta
tell you?, he chides his charges, who fall splayed
and spring back up, nimble as spiders.

Who knew his badass sport — jubilant nights
in parking garages, vaulting stairs and landing
wheels down, knees bent —

who knew it would come to this, moms in mini-skirts
flipping open laptops in the Parent Lounge peppered
with signs: *Sorry, we no longer accept $100 bills.*

What happened to his dream, his sweet, concrete dream?
Who could have foreseen the bedlam, big-name skaters
emblazoned with logos and posturing like rock stars —

how did he get stuck with crowd control, kids shoving
to get their helmets, boards and arms signed, some already
shaving, but too pleased with their souvenir
to hide it —

and why should they deny their allegiance
to denizens of the sport's hypnotic geometry, body
perpendicular to the board, iconic as a sundial
and gliding with loose, effortless grace
on the polished slab of pressed
carbon fiber —

even as it corkscrews, as gloved palm slaps down
on sizzling asphalt, skaters claiming their place
in parking lots and strip malls from Hempstead
to Mineola to the suburbs of Jersey and Ohio,

their legacy shifting west, rural route unfurling
as some farm kid works the momentum fueling
her longboard, Cadillac of the industry,
big wheels built for low,

lazy gliding, groundhogs snuffling along the shoulder
as she lifts her arms, dips and rises, deep knee
bends coaxing velocity's shy strength
to show itself, again.

The Meat Paradox: Why People Can Love Animals — And Eat Them

I wouldn't want his hands in my mouth, that dentist
from Minnesota grinning in safari gear, staggering
with the weight of Cecil the Lion's head,

black mane sticky with blood and jaws agape,
fangs like scissors — while the dentist's teeth
are movie-star white, and he's tanned

in a recreational way, like Ted Bundy,
who hacksawed the heads from his victims
and displayed them, sorrowful and vacant,
in his apartment.

When park rangers found Cecil's skinned,
headless body, his tracking collar was missing.

Maybe it sits angled under accent lighting
on the dentist's mantel, positioned next to the arrow
he shot between Cecil's ribs and which stayed
lodged there, as he staggered across
the grasslands, bleeding out.

Protesters chanted *Murderer* outside the dentist's
split-level, suburban home. They spray-painted
Lion Killer in red letters, on his white
garage door.

A woman tweeted: *Why doesn't a bucket
of chicken wings, evoke the same rage?*

Everything I Know About Forgiveness, I Learned From My Dog

Her breed is trained to hunt wild boars in red clay
ravines, moss draped on scrub oak and fog erasing
the mangroves' leathery leaves.

Puppies chase a raccoon trapped in a mesh barrel,
bouncing down a hill. They lunge and nip at a boarlet
in a harness tethered to a tree, so young he has
chipmunk stripes down his back, squealing
for the sow shot earlier that day.

I toss my dog's fake prey across the room.
The squirrel has orange eyes and a squeaker
in its tail. The beaver's belly is torn flaps I stuff
with crumpled paper for the thrilling,
crinkly sound.

My dog is an apex predator who sleeps on a foam bed.
She neither flushes nor retrieves target mammals.
She sniffs the sidewalk for Goldfish crackers
thrown from a stroller. She looks to me

for approval and tracks my mood like the child
of an alcoholic — shrewd, watchful, driven
by self-preservation and a hunger to belong.

You Are Made of Stardust

A power line is out of sorts, electric buzz slicing

through the haze of dusk, every living thing

the target of ions in a beeline for somewhere else.

We are the meat that exploded stars pass through.

I don't know where I end and the city begins.

I gave you my story and the story under that.

I am free as a comet. I am made of ice. I melt.

Why Starting Over Can Be the Best Thing for You

The frog's heart generates a gel that grips
its organs like anti-freeze. In spring,
the frog thaws from the inside
out, and blinks.

Every winter that passes, is a triumph.
I clench my gut, carry longing for the sun
like an egg in my throat.
I start over. I blink.

Everything Looks Better in the Fleeting Beauty of the Golden Hour

I might not seize the day, but I savor the late afternoon
perfect for outdoor shoots, silhouettes gold-leafed
with sun. It's the time cocktails are mixed, amber
poured into a chunky crystal glass, a woman
in a voluminous white gown posed between Doric columns
framing the Hudson, her face golden, her long train golden
as it cascades down marble stairs. It's that magic hour
before dusk when the pale walls of my apartment are brushed
with gold, and I'm dancing in the living room, my dog
watching with the soft eyes of love.

Acknowledgments

I'm sending special thanks to the very creative and discerning team at Broadstone Books: Larry W. Moore, Stephanie Potter, Sheila Bucy Potter, Morgan Saylor, Samantha Ratcliffe, Jeremy Wooldridge, Ashley Johnson and Eileen Bunch. Here's a big hug of gratitude to the weekly writing group I joined 12 years ago: Susana H. Case, Elizabeth Haukaas, Myra Malkin and Hilary Sideris. Much respect and affection for my co-hosts who have helped keep the West-East Poets of the Pandemic and Beyond (W-E) reading series alive these past five years: Susana H. Case, Carolyne Wright and Sandy Yannone, as well as early W-E host, William Mohr—and here's a nostalgic shout out and super big hug to Gerry LaFemina, who invited me to join him in hosting the very much in-person, NYC Lunar Walk Poetry Series in 2012, with co-hosts Madeleine Barnes and Bryn Dodson turning up the dial as we powered through to 2020. Finally, much love to my family, especially the little ones: Alistair, Bryce, Reya, Teo and Willow, who stand on the cusp of this pivotal moment for humanity and every living thing. With words and actions, we all play a part in protecting what they will inherit.

Much gratitude to these journals in which these poems previously appeared:

Asheville Poetry Review: "Betrayal Is Behind the Spread of Humans Around the World"

Atlanta Review: "Scientists Have Finally Found Out Why People Love Each Other" (as "Wolfram, my Valentine")

Atticus Review: "Bioluminescence Can Be Ours"

Bonanza by Lynn McGee, winner of the Slapering Hol Press chapbook contest: "Animals Will Take Over the Earth, After We Eradicate Ourselves" (as "Dropping a Wasp in Deep Snow")

Glassworks: "What's Really Holding You Back?" (as "Zoo Dream")

North Dakota Quarterly: "Longing Comes to Life: Mary Wollstonecraft Shelley Reflects on a Life Well Lived" (as "Longing Comes to Life")

Oberon Magazine: "Everything I Know About Forgiveness, I Learned From my Dog" (as "How to Raise a Predator")

Rogue Agent: "Biking It Off"

San Pedro River Review: "Tell Me One More Time, What to Do About Grief"

Slant: "Sweet Concrete Dream: Skate Culture Transcends Sellout Culture" (as "Sweet Concrete Dream")

Tampa Review: "Bathing the Dog"

Westchester Review: "What Animals Can Teach Us About Being Human" and "The Meat Paradox: Why People Can Love Animals — And Eat Them"

About the Author

Lynn McGee is the author of *Science Says Yes* and *Tracks*, both with Broadstone Books, as well as *Sober Cooking* (Spuyten Duyvil Press), and two award-winning poetry chapbooks: *Heirloom Bulldog* (Bright Hill Press) and *Bonanza* (Slapering Hol Press). Her poems have been published widely in journals and anthologies. She is co-author with José Pelauz of the children's book *Starting Over in Sunset Park* (Tilbury House Press). Lynn earned an MFA in Poetry at Columbia University School of the Arts and taught in private and public colleges, secondary schools, and literacy programs before becoming a communications manager at Borough of Manhattan Community College, The City University of New York. For more information, visit www.lynnmcgee.com.